CONQUEST *of the* ATLANTIC

CUNARD LINERS OF THE 1950s AND 1960s

WILLIAM H. MILLER

FONTHILL

For Maureen Ryan

a gracious, wonderful dear friend, and the epitome of Cunard staff

Opposite: The majestic *Queen Mary*, perhaps the most beloved Cunarder of all, arriving at New York in 1957. (*Moran Towing & Transportation Co.*)

Fonthill Media Limited
Fonthill Media LLC
www.fonthillmedia.com
office@fonthillmedia.com

First published in the United Kingdom and the United States of America 2014

British Library Cataloguing in Publication Data:
A catalogue record for this book is available from the British Library

Copyright © William H. Miller 2014

ISBN 978-1-78155-350-3

The right of William H. Miller to be identified as the author of this work has been asserted by him in accordance with the Copyright, Designs and Patents Act 1988.

Typeset in Minion Pro 11pt on 15pt
Printed and bound in England

CONTENTS

FOREWORD

I felt very honoured when Bill Miller asked me to write a foreword for his new book on Cunard and their transatlantic liners. We first met years ago on the *QE2* when I was a social hostess and many voyages and books later, he still enthrals, capturing the magic and mystique of the transatlantic voyage.

For me, they were so special to any other voyage, a liner setting out across the vast Atlantic for days in a no man's land, like being between two worlds. So many memories and images such as one quiet afternoon on *Queen Elizabeth* at the end of the glamorous era of transatlantic travel when I was a lady assistant purser. A slight dark-haired passenger crossed 'A Deck Square' in front of the Purser's Office. One of the great Hollywood stars, I stood admiring her beautiful profile. Then the legend that is Elizabeth Taylor turned and was gone.

The *Queens* crossed the Atlantic all year and I recall walking along the chilly enclosed Promenade Deck on *Queen Mary*. The winter Atlantic was grey but icy smooth, passengers in deckchairs wrapped in steamer rugs, and then stepping back into the warmth of the ship, the string quartet playing Cole Porter during afternoon tea in the Main Lounge.

And just before *Queen Elizabeth* went out of service, I sat with the chief deck steward on the Promenade Deck, helping him sew the ship's paying-off pennant for her final voyage with Cunard. I remember seeing it flying from the mast, one foot for every year of service, swirling and twirling in the wind—it looked to me like the ship was waving goodbye.

And the beloved *QE2* in May 1982. The ship arrived from Philadelphia and docked in Southampton one early afternoon. I sat in the cruise director's quarters, sharing an end of voyage drink with a guest lecturer, actor Larry Hagman—enjoying a break from *Dallas*—and his wife, when a member of staff rushed in, having just picked up the news on BBC radio. The *QE2* had been commissioned as a troopship for the conflict in the Falklands. Our lovely ship, as many other Cunarders before her, had been called to duty and was 'STUFT' ('Ship Taken up from Trade').

22 December 2003: I was in the Grand Lobby and heard the announcement, 'All visitors are requested to disembark as *Queen Mary 2* will shortly be sailing from St Nazaire.' This magnificent 150,000-ton liner had been handed over that day and was now officially part of the Cunard family, ready to meet the world. Hundreds of crew lined the decks in cold afternoon sunshine, the crowds ashore thronged to watch her passage to the open sea, cheering and waving from both sides, as another Cunard transatlantic liner went into service.

Over the years working for Cunard, I always felt so privileged to be part of the great ships, their history and traditions—may they long continue.

MAUREEN RYAN
Ex-Social Hostess
Cunard Line

ACKNOWLEDGEMENTS

Like the hardworking crews of Cunard liners, it takes many hands to create a book by assembling materials, gathering photographs, collecting anecdotes and recollections. It is an assembly process and as author, I am something of the Chief Purser.

Foremost thanks to Jay Slater and Alan Sutton at Fonthill Media for taking on this project. They have been exceptional as working partners. Special appreciation to Maureen Ryan for her evocative foreword and to Brenton Jenkins, Len Houghton and Robert Welding for their outstanding recollections, impressions, insights and tales. Added special thanks to Michael Hadgis for his technical support.

Valued anecdotes and recollections came from Robert Aldridge, Jack Allyn, the late John Malcolm Brinnin, the late Arthur Crook, John Ferguson, David Gibson, Richard Gibson, the late Lewis Gordon, Mary Horan, James Moran, John Savage, William Smith, Philippe Spanner, Arthur Taylor, John Whitworth, the late Captain Robin Woodall, and the late Everett Viez.

Photograph resources include Ernest Arroyo, Philippe Brebant, Michael Cassar, Luis Miguel Correia, the late Frank Cronican, Richard Faber, the late John Gillespie, the late Andrew Kilk, Anthony La Forgia, Michael D. J. Lennon, Richard K. Morse, Tim Noble, David Powers, Richard Turnwald, Richard Weiss and Albert Wilhelmi.

Companies and organisations that have helped include the Cunard Line, Moran Towing & Transportation Co., National Geographic Society, Port Authority of New York & New Jersey, South China Morning Post Ltd, Southern Newspapers Ltd, Steamship Historical Society of America, World Ocean & Cruise Liner Society and World Ship Society.

INTRODUCTION

As a boy who was fascinated by the great ocean liners, I kept a shoebox filled with postcards, a drawer of brochures and, mostly rolled up in a back corner of a closet, those large posters. One of my favourites was an aerial view of the Cunard fleet as it was in 1957—the biggest in the Atlantic! What a collection of ships and very beautiful ships at that. There were the *Queens*, *Mauretania*, *Caronia* and *Britannic* in the lead positions, then the *Saxonia*, *Ivernia*, *Carinthia* and *Sylvania*, and finally the *Media*, *Parthia* and *Scythia*.

The company motto read: 'Getting there was half the fun.' And Cunard offered more sailings—sometimes as many as four in a week from New York—of all transatlantic companies.

Seeing, say, the *Queen Elizabeth*, the *Mauretania* or the all-green *Caronia* sail along the Hudson was pure ocean liner romance. They hinted at power, size, faraway destinations and the sense that liners were indeed like floating cities. I also visited many Cunarders on those pre-sailing occasions at Piers 90 and 92, and well recall the dazzling interiors, glossy woods, artworks, thick carpets and highly polished lino floors. We would pass through the vast lounges, smoking rooms and restaurants, and sometimes poke our noses for a quick look into the staterooms and suites. There were fresh flowers in the public rooms, monogrammed ashtrays on tables and writing rooms with stacks of stationery and postcards. There might even be live music being played in a main lounge. Then, of course, there were the hustle and bustle of the outbound passengers and attending staff. It was all very exciting, all very impressionable, and all magic!

I have been most fortunate to gather the recollections of some staff members which altogether add life and personality to these otherwise mostly bygone Cunarders. I still meet passengers aboard the current day Cunard liners that sailed, say, fifty and even sixty years ago aboard the likes of the *Queen Mary*, *Britannic* and *Carinthia*. Often, they are excited and happy to share impressions, recollections and cherished memories. Ashore, Cunard remains a giant to ocean liner collectors and enthusiasts.

On the eve of Cunard's 175th anniversary in 2015, I am happy to add this collection of histories and memories of the last generation of company liners on the North Atlantic. Cunard, it seems, gave us so much. But for now, a Cunarder is sailing from Manhattan's West Side. Passengers line the decks and well-wishers fill the pier. Streamers are being tossed and, most evocatively, a deep, throaty whistle sounds—again and again. Hopefully, this book is something of a reminder of those golden times.

BILL MILLER
Secaucus, New Jersey, US
April 2014

Chapter One

CUNARD

A Brief History of a Proud Company

Few maritime companies have a richer history. The history of the Cunard Line—the once Liverpool-based Cunard Steam-Ship Company Limited—is practically the history of the entire North Atlantic passenger ship trade. Cunard dominated, but also competed, innovated and built some of the most significant passenger ships of all time. They also taught us what an ocean liner looked like.

Cunard began in 1839 by a Nova Scotia ship-owner, Samuel Cunard. Together with three partners, he luckily obtained the prized mail contract to America from the British Admiralty. Quickly, he ordered four new packet steamers. The first of these, the 1,100-ton *Britannia* sailed from Liverpool to Boston in July 1840. The crossing took fourteen days and Cunard was officially in business.

By 1900, the Cunard transatlantic service—sailing to New York as well as Boston and Eastern Canada—was highly profitable and very popular. Cunard ships were known for their great reliability, punctuality and splendid British service. The company's ships seemed always to be in the news as well. It was aboard the *Laconia* in 1901 that Marconi carried out his first practical experiments with wireless telegraphy. Two years later, the same ship published the very first onboard newspaper for its passengers. Updated news was transmitted by daily wireless reports. Another Cunarder, the *Carpathia*, achieved maritime immortality when it rescued 705 survivors from the ill-fated *Titanic* in April 1912.

Cunard almost always owned and operated statistically important ships as well. In 1907, the company commissioned the world's largest and fastest superliners, the 32,000-ton *Mauretania* and *Lusitania*. In 1914, an even bigger and more luxurious liner was introduced: the 45,000-ton *Aquitania*. In the 1920s, Cunard operated what they dubbed 'the Big Three'—*Mauretania, Aquitania* and *Berengaria*.

It was in the otherwise hard-pressed 1930s that Cunard created two of the world's most extraordinary vessels, the incomparable queens, the 81,000-ton *Queen Mary* and 83,000-ton *Queen Elizabeth*. They would run the Atlantic's first weekly and two-ship service, and in doing so, would become the most successful and famous pair of liners ever built. Even their successor, the 66,000-ton *Queen Elizabeth 2* that sailed for thirty-nine years, became the most successful superliner of all time.

During the Second World War, Cunarders gave heroic, valiant and highly valuable service. Alone, the *Queens* transported over two million wartime passengers. The company also lost thirty-six ships. Consequently, the end of the war in the summer of 1945 was a time for renewal and rebuilding. Cunard had to re-establish its position on the reawakening, but fiercely competitive transatlantic shipping trade.

It was business as usual. With a shortage of tonnage, the first sailings in the winter of 1946–47 of the newly refitted *Queen Elizabeth* were booked to capacity. A year later in the summer of 1947, Cunard's *Media* was ranked as the first new Atlantic passenger ship built since 1939. Post-war Cunard was soon trading at full capacity, high popularity and with great profit.

Chapter Two

THE QUEENS

The Legendary Mary and Elizabeth

Horns hooted, sirens blared and flags fluttered on a November day in 1946. In the revived high spirits of post-war New York City, its harbour laid on a royal welcome—the freshly restored *Queen Elizabeth* was arriving on her commercial maiden voyage. She was the largest liner ever built, had a heroic war image, but was over six years late. She had been due on her maiden voyage in April 1940, but the outbreak of war changed all that. First, the 83,673-gross-ton liner had to serve the Allied cause, sailing as a grey-painted troopship from the Suez to Ceylon, to Australia, San Francisco, and most of all, crossing and re-crossing the Atlantic between New York and Gourock in Scotland. The *Queen Elizabeth* was one of the most famous, proud and heroic liners of all time.

Running a weekly Atlantic service with the *Queens*, two fast and large liners, was an idea that emerged in the 1920s at Cunard's stately Liverpool headquarters. The 81,000-ton ship that became the *Queen Mary* was to run with White Star Line's proposed 60,000-ton *Oceanic*. But the idea of the *Oceanic* died with the onset of the Great Depression in October 1929. Cunard had to build its own second ship. They were prompted by financial support from the British Government, their own profit, replacement of older Cunard liners (large ships such as the *Mauretania*, *Aquitania* and *Berengaria*) and national as well as corporate prestige. The Germans, Italians and, most enviously, the French were building new superliners that would carry and show the flag in America.

Much has been written about the creation and building of the *Queens*. Therefore, suffice to simply say that while the first of the pair was delayed in construction by just over two years (December 1931–April 1934), the *Queen Mary* was finally named and launched in September 1934. She entered service in May 1936 to great acclaim, rousing headlines and enormous success (she enjoyed a highly enviable 98 per cent occupancy factor by 1939). She was the pride of the British fleet, immediately creating a special bond with passengers and crew alike, and reigned as the fastest liner afloat (from 1938 until the advent of the *United States* in 1952).

The second ship, slightly larger, more modern and contemporary, and statistically the largest ship afloat, the *Queen Elizabeth*—due in Southampton–New York service in April 1940—was delayed by the dramatic start of the Second World War in Europe in September 1939. The incomplete *Queen Elizabeth*, and painted in grey, fled to New York for safety in March 1940. She had been scheduled for a celebratory commercial maiden voyage that April, thereby creating the two-ship express service and highlighting Cunard's 100th anniversary.

Opposite page, clockwise from top:
The giant *Queen Mary 2* docked in Sydney for the first time in February 2007. (*Author's collection*)

The *Queen Mary* is in the centre while the *Queen Elizabeth* has just arrived in the safety of still-neutral America. The date is 7 March 1940. The *Normandie* is to the left. (*Cronican-Arroyo collection*)

During the war, the *Queens* had capacities for 15,000 troops. (*Albert Wilhelmi collection*)

There were other more important and urgent duties for the *Queens*—to be used as 15,000-capacity Allied troopships. Used on the North Atlantic, ferrying their soldier passengers between New York and Gourock (Southampton was off limits during the war), they became the most heroic and valiant ocean liners of all time. By the war's end, Churchill said that the work of the *Queens* helped cut the war in Europe by at least a year. Together, they delivered over 2,000,000 military passengers. The *Queen Mary* established the greatest record for any ship when she departed from Manhattan's Pier 90 with 16,683 passengers onboard.

Right: In grey paint, the *Queen Mary* at war: a heroic and valiant ship. (*Richard Faber collection*)

Below: Moving along the lower Hudson River, the *Queen Mary* arrives in this view from December 1959. (*Richard K. Morse collection*)

Above: Three Cunarders will be departing within twenty-four hours on crossings—the *Mauretania*, *Queen Mary* and *Britannic*. (*Port Authority of New York & New Jersey*)

Right: The *Queen Mary* passes Lower Manhattan, making for a 9.00 a.m. arrival at Pier 90. (*Port Authority of New York & New Jersey*)

The *Queens* were decommissioned from military service in 1946—the refitted *Queen Elizabeth* finally had her commercial maiden voyage in November 1946; the restored *Queen Mary* followed in July 1947. Business boomed almost from the start. In the ensuing years, the *Queens* would greatly benefit the war-torn British economy. Alone, they would deliver thousands of tourists, mostly money-spending Americans, to British shores. They were the most successful pair of transatlantic liners ever created. For about ten months of the year, they ran a very steady, reliable, mostly comfortable and often luxurious relay across the 'great pond'—five days in each direction between New York, Cherbourg and Southampton. If the *Queen Mary* was

sailing from New York on Wednesday, then the *Queen Elizabeth* was heading westbound from Southampton and Cherbourg on Thursday. Then, two-and-a-half days later, they would pass one another in the North Atlantic—and often in viewing range—at a combined speed of some 57 knots. Two of the most important passenger ships ever built must have made an incredible spectacle.

James Moran, a native of Liverpool, served aboard the *Queen Elizabeth* and *Queen Mary* in the 1950s. We met in his later career as a hotel manager aboard the deluxe eighty-eight passenger cruising yacht *Renaissance III*. He had fond memories of those three-class Cunard super ships. 'The *Queens* were a way of getting to your destination.

No less than six Moran tugs will assist the *Queen Mary* in docking at Pier 90, West 50th Street. (*Moran Towing & Transportation Co.*)

2,246 passengers
$65,000 worth of express cargo
649 bags of mail
Thirty-four diplomatic pouches
1,500 bon voyage parcels
1,689 pieces of heavy baggage
8,992 pieces of stateroom baggage
Twenty-six cars
113 containers of movie film
479 bars of gold bullion (valued at $490,000)
Fourteen dogs
Nine cats
Three birds
One monkey

These two ships and their sailings were transport—transport in its highest form. Today's cruise ships are "fun ships" that provide a moving vacation. The ports are not destinations, but diversions. Even the passengers were very different back then. Aboard the *Queens,* especially in first class, they often travelled with enormous amounts and pieces of luggage including some of those now all but vanished steamer trunks.'

Each five-day crossing onboard the *Queen Elizabeth* as well as the *Queen Mary* were done with regularity and precision, but were also enormously complicated and detailed affairs. As an example, on a voyage from New York to Cherbourg and Southampton in 1955, the *Queen Elizabeth* had an extensive, but quite customary manifest (above).

Sailing days at Cunard's Pier 90 and 92 in New York, especially Wednesdays, were big, busy, festive events. They were often memorable. Beginning three hours before actual sailing time, which varied for the *Queens* due to the Hudson River tides, passengers boarded through separate gangways and were divided by class. Visitors who paid fifty cents to aid the Seamen's Fund boarded separately. Sailings drew huge crowds—if 2,000 passengers were departing on a sailing in high summer aboard, say, the *Queen Mary*, there might be as many as 5,000 visitors. Everyone, including the visitors, was dressed in formal daytime attire: neckties and business suits for the men, dresses, gloves and fur wraps for the women. Everyone, it seemed, wore hats. Bon voyage parties, either in public rooms or more likely in cabins, were the norm. There was Champagne, canapés and often, usually a sailing gift, one of those great wicker baskets of fresh fruit and wrapped in yellow-orange cellophane.

Departing from the north side of Pier 90. (*Richard Faber collection*)

Robert Aldridge recalled a Cunard crossing. 'I was on the third crossing after the *Queen Mary*'s post-war refit in September 1947. The weather was awful. Everybody was sick. We were going to America, to New York. It was the biggest event of my entire life. I was then eight years old!'

'My grandparents took my brother and I to Europe in the summer of 1956,' remembered William Smith. 'We sailed over in June on the *Queen Mary* and returned in late August on the *Queen Elizabeth*. We were in first class. Danny Kaye was aboard on the trip going over and Joan Fontaine on the return.'

Among Cunard staff, there were differences and preferences especially between the *Queens*. Long-time purser Brenton Jenkins preferred the *Queen Mary*. 'She was my very favourite Cunard ship, although I spent almost equal time between the *Mary* and *Lizzie*. The latter and much newer built was considered by Cunard Liverpool headquarters to be the commodore ship with the Commodore Captain of the Line in Command and the Senior Chief Purser, Lionel Carine, who was there from the beginning until her final ending and his retirement. I always thought the *Lizzie* had a utility look about her, especially in all her first-class public rooms and cabins. There were nothing of those beautiful and lavishly appointed public rooms and first-class cabins in the *Queen Mary*. The *Mary* also had very many wonderful and large art paintings throughout the rooms while the *Lizzie* had practically none. When I look at pictures today of the first-class restaurant and main lounge, and other public rooms of the *Mary*,

Majestically passing West 42nd Street and the midtown Manhattan skyline. (*Author's collection*)

Clockwise from top left:
Midday arrival in New York in April 1962. (*ALF collection*)
The beautiful *Queen Elizabeth* departing from the King George V graving dock at Southampton. (*Cunard*)
Film star Eleanor Parker creates the perfect pose aboard the inbound *Queen Mary* at New York. (*Cunard*)

and remember from my memory banks and compare them to the *Lizzie*, its chalk and cheese. There's no comparison. The first-class dining room on the *Lizzie* was the largest room ever built on a ship in those days seating 800 passengers, however.

'A superlative room, three decks high with walls and supporting columns covered in beautiful veneers of woods from around the world and all with ceiling lighting panels to give a restful ambiance to the diners. The four forward main entrance doors were bronze cast and the work of father and son designers Gilberts. They were manned at all meals by bellboys to open and shut for the passenger. Above these entrance doors was a painted panel up to the ceiling and down the sides of the doors, "Merrie England" by Philip Connard, and executed in a faux-tapestry technique. I knew these things because I had to make a BBC television programme at one time covering these facts and details. On the aft central wall of the room and covering the whole wall was the ocean map showing the two crossing routes, west and eastbound, and with crystal replicas of both ships, automatically moveable into their daily positions.

'There was a smaller one in the first-class smoke room, which was more or less a male-dominated room. The white table cloths, cutlery, glassware and China were of the very finest quality and there were fresh flowers decorating every table. It was such a lovely sight to see the dining room all laid out and the waiters perfectly dressed in their uniforms all ready to receive their passengers before the opening of the restaurant doors. It was truly an outstanding room and a sight to behold when filled at night with beautifully dressed and bejewelled ladies and the men all in their dinner jackets. There was no such grander scene anywhere ashore or afloat. I hosted a

Aboard the *Queen Mary*. From top to bottom:
Strolling the boat deck was a favourite pastime on Cunarders. (*Author's collection*)

Art deco on the high seas: the imposing main lounge in first class. (*Author's collection*)

The chic Verandah Grill. (*Author's collection*)

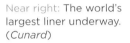

large round passenger table every night amongst it all. The first-class cabins had the same luxury standards with a telephone manned by a large ship's switchboard of lady telephonists with European and American contact twenty-four hours a day. In all my life travelling around the world and visiting of many famous hotels and sailing on many ships, I have never come across a more beautiful room or scene—and I am sure I never will.'

Mary Horan added, 'My father was very proud to work for Cunard, joining in 1948. He worked on many of their ships, but was especially proud to serve aboard the *Queen Mary* and *Queen Elizabeth*. My mother had dinner waiting for him at home in December 1964. My father was late, it seemed, and then did not phone. The ship was being overhauled in the local Harland and Wolff dockyard at Southampton and my father was part of the small Cunard crew. It seems he had fallen down a dark stairwell, had a massive brain injury and died rather quickly. He had been taken to a local hospital and formally pronounced dead before my mother was even called. It was a sad accident, of course, but my father died where he wanted to be. He just loved the *Queens*.'

'Back in the 1950s, a waiter on the *Queens* earned about thirty dollars a week,' concluded James Moran. 'But tips were very good because of the heavy loads of Americans. They were often incredibly generous. Other British passenger liners such as P&O and Union-Castle were not known for their excessively high tips.'

Top: The starboard gallery, also in first class. (*Author's collection*)

Above: Dining splendour: the main restaurant in first class. (*Author's collection*)

Left: More celebrity passengers travelled on Cunard in the 1950s. Film star Ginger Rogers is posed along the boat deck. (*Cunard*)

Not every crewmember was as loyal and devoted. 'I was a dishwasher in the galley aboard the *Queen Elizabeth* in the late 1950s,' recalled John Savage. 'It was a tough job. But late at night, after the second dinner, we'd toss some of the plates out of the galley portholes. We were tired and we washed enough dishes. To this day, I think the North Atlantic must be littered with Cunard China!'

Len Houghton was the senior barkeep on the cruise ship *Cunard Countess* when we met in 1983 and was one of the most senior staff members with Cunard. He had joined back in 1935, beginning as a fifteen-year-old bellboy. 'When I joined Cunard-White Star as it was then known, it was a very great honour to work for them. They were the most illustrious and distinguished steamship firm in the world,' he reflected. 'I was first assigned to the *Laurentic*, one of the White Star Line ships that had come over in the merger with Cunard in 1934. We were running "Depression Cruises" to the Mediterranean, sailing from Southampton, London and Liverpool for as little as four to five dollars a day. I was aboard the *Laurentic* on 18 August 1935 when we were rammed in the Irish Sea by the Blue Star Line freighter *Napier Star*. It was a miserable collision. Six of our boys were killed. Soon after, the *Laurentic* (built in 1927) was laid up and was all but finished off except for emergency sailings. I was then reassigned to *Andania*, one of Cunard's own 13,000-tonners used on the Canadian run. Caused by the Depression, she had just finished a long spell of lay-up at Falmouth. Cunard, like so many others, had too few passengers. When I joined the *Andania*, she had grass growing on her foredecks.'

After serving on numerous Cunard ships during the heroic and perilous days of the Second World War, Houghton had yet to work on the *Queen Elizabeth*. 'In the late 1940s and 1950s, Cunard ran a deluxe transatlantic shuttle,' he added. 'It was indeed still the Palm Court days. We could cater for any nationality and in first class a full breakfast could be ordered and then promptly served at three in the afternoon. Of course, the old *Queen Mary* was the most favoured ship by passengers as well as crews. She had the grandest atmosphere, but also a unique and almost undefinable "magic chemistry" with those onboard her.'

sail away to Europe on Cunard's **VACATION ISLAND**

What's *your* idea of a vacation? Dancing, swimming, fine food? A chance to relax and be waited on hand and foot? Meet new people, get some fresh sea air into your lungs? Escape from the nerve-fraying tensions of supersonic daily life? Well, look no further! Each sailing of Cunard's ten Vacation Islands—headed by the stabilizer-equipped superliners Queen Elizabeth and Queen Mary—includes *your* kind of vacation in the cost of the transportation. A perfectly relaxed way to begin and end a pleasure or business trip to Europe. You owe it to yourself to discover the timeless offerings of these sophisticated resorts-at-sea. An average of three weekly Cunard sailings from New York and throughout the year . . . which means . . . season *you* choose!

Getting there is half the fun . . . GO
CUNARD
QUEEN ELIZABETH • QUEEN MARY
MAURETANIA • CARONIA • SYLVANIA • MEDIA
PARTHIA • CARINTHIA • IVERNIA • SAXONIA

Over 50,000 years of experience are behind each thoughtful act when you go Cunard

When you ring for service aboard a Cunarder, you ring for experience. And tradition. And thoughtfulness. Of more than 8,000 men and women aboard Cunard ships, the majority are stewards, stewardesses, waiters and other catering personnel dedicated to serve you. They offer an aggregate of over 50,000 years at sea . . . and almost half of them have had between 10 and 45 years of training and experience. But a bond stronger than time in uniform unites them. Pride in a job well done is the real reason for Cunard's 119-year success on the Atlantic . . . that and a seagoing tradition which causes sons to follow fathers and grandfathers in Cunard service. Behind the slogan, "Getting There is Half the Fun," are the thousands of men and women who make it so on every crossing.

Getting there is half the fun . . . Go **CUNARD**

Widest choice of ships, rates, and sailings from New York and Canada to Europe. Consult your travel agent or Cunard Line. Main office in U.S.—25 Broadway, New York, N. Y.

QUEEN ELIZABETH • QUEEN MARY • MAURETANIA • CARONIA • BRITANNIC • MEDIA • PARTHIA • CARINTHIA • IVERNIA • SAXONIA • SYLVANIA

Top: An advertisement dated 1956. (*National Geographic Society*)

Left: An advertisement dated November 1959. (*National Geographic Society*)

Clockwise from above:
Summer morning in 1958 with the *Queen Elizabeth* at the top and then the *Olympia*, *United States*, *America*, *Independence* and *Vulcania*. (*Port Authority of New York & New Jersey*)

July 1961 as the *Queen Elizabeth* arrives with (from left to right) *Independence*, *America*, *United States*, *Olympia*, the aircraft carrier USS *Intrepid*, *Mauretania* and *Sylvania*. (*Port Authority of New York & New Jersey*)

A glorious if sad farewell to New York in October 1968. (*Author's collection*)

During a cruise in the mid 1960s, the *Queen Elizabeth* is seen at Cristobal with the *United States*. (Author's Collection)

It lasted for six happy years for me and I continued afterward in the modern cruise industry with Royal Caribbean of Miami until my eventual retirement in 1995.'

In the 1960s, John Whitworth was a director and the managing director of the historic Cunard Line. In 1965, the company was still the largest, if not the busiest, on the North Atlantic run. 'Getting there was still half the fun, if less and less appealing on five to eight day ocean liner crossings. Lumbering on, there were the increasingly dowdy *Queens*, the original *Queen Mary* and *Queen Elizabeth* as well as the *Mauretania*, *Caronia*, *Carmania*, *Franconia*, *Carinthia* and *Sylvania*. But time was running out and running out all too quickly as the decisive airlines and their jetliners drew more and more passengers. Cunard was losing over five million dollars a year to the airlines. Increasingly apparent, crossings were all but over and cruising was the future. However, while the *Queen Mary* was retired in 1967, Cunard planned—and with great if misguided hopes—that a new Atlantic superliner could be built to sail in a weekly tandem with the ageing and refitted *Queen Elizabeth*. The new liner project, a creation of early 1960s enthusiasm, was dubbed the *Q3* project

'We had our first meetings in October 1961 to plan for the *Q3*, the replacement for the then twenty-five-year-old *Queen Mary*. Cunard was then still a very conservative, very British, very old fashioned company. Their Liverpool headquarters was a commercial palace, but was dubbed the "Kremlin" by everyone in middle management. Top management was absolutely dictatorial. But the *Q3* was the wrong design and she was a rather traditional ship in many ways. The British side of Cunard wanted two classes whereas, rather unexpectedly, the New York office still pushed for the traditional three classes: first, cabin and tourist. The whole idea and the entire design were soon scrapped. The *Q3* design was redone and became the *Q4,* which in turn became the *Queen Elizabeth 2*. The British Government, after much wooing by Cunard, provided a sixty million dollar loan. Shipyards began to bid after the design was first announced in December 1962. In the end, John Brown on the Clyde in Scotland got the order with some politics in play

The Queen Elizabeth outbound at New York for the last time in October 1968. (*Gillespie-Faber Collection*)

as well and this was made public on 30 December 1964. (Among others, John Brown's shipyard had built the likes of the *Lusitania*, *Aquitania*, *Queen Mary* and *Queen Elizabeth*.)

'Plans for the *Q4* were reworked and then reworked again and again,' added Whitworth. 'At the same time, there was new, fresh management coming aboard at Cunard. The dust was gradually blown away and a new team of forty year olds were in place. There was even a new, enlightened and very contemporary design team. Captain William Warwick was appointed the first master of the new ship (65,000 tons at best estimates of the day) and the plan was to operate her with the older, but larger *Elizabeth*. However, there was a devastating British maritime strike in May and June of 1966. Cruelly, it lasted six weeks and like other shipping lines, Cunard lost something close to fifteen million dollars. And as the jetliners made even deeper inroads, plans were changed—the old *Queen Elizabeth* was out (sold off in 1968) and the new *Q4* would operate in tandem with a former competitor, the French Line and their four-year-old *France*.'

Whitworth was later placed in charge of selling off the thirty-one-year-old *Queen Mary* in 1967 and the twenty-eight-year-old *Queen Elizabeth* the following year. Faded and rusting, they were still two of the most famous liners ever built and the *Queen Elizabeth* was the largest liner yet to go to sea. 'I sold the much loved *Queen Mary* for three-and-a-half million dollars in cash to the City of Long Beach in California,' he recounted. 'The *Queen Elizabeth* went a year later, but for seven-and-a-half million dollars to Philadelphia buyers, but mostly on credit. Cunard lost lots of money on that transaction.'

The two giant *Queens* had suddenly turned into aged anachronisms and huge dinosaurs by the time the jets arrived in full force in the early 1960s. In the end, there were instances of the *Queen Elizabeth* arriving in New York with 200 to 300 passengers, but still being looked after by 1,200 crewmembers. James Moran lamented their passing—the *Queen Mary* to southern California for further use as a hotel/museum and the *Queen Elizabeth* to a fiery end, sinking and then demolition in a Hong Kong harbour. He concluded, 'The whole transatlantic era disappeared very suddenly, almost overnight. Then everyone scrambled to write about it, to recount the passing of a magnificent era. Even now, I can't believe that it is all gone. But I am very proud to have been a part of such a time.'

The illustrious and much loved *Queen Mary* was retired from Cunard service in September 1967. After over 1,000 crossings, she was given a well-deserved final and often tearful send off from New York. Her fate might have been as a migrant ship on the UK–Australia run, a moored casino at Gibraltar or even as a high school docked in New York harbour. But the City of Long Beach, California—

Top: War had just started in Europe when this photo was taken in September 1939. Showing (from top to bottom) *Monarch of Bermuda, Rex, Aquitania, Queen Mary* (both in grey colouring), *Normandie* and *Ile de France*. (*Port Authority of New York & New Jersey*)

Left: The British maritime strike of May–June 1966 showing the laid-up *Queen Mary* in centre position; the *Pendennis Castle* and *Caronia* on the top; and at the bottom, the *Franconia* and *Andes*. (*Southern Newspapers Ltd*)

Left: The *Queen Mary* seen on her final night in New York on 21 September 1967. (*Cronican-Arroyo collection*)

Right: The *Queen Mary* leaves Pier 92 and Luxury Liner Row for the last time on 22 September 1967. (*Port Authority of New York & New Jersey*)

Left: The *Queen Mary 2* meets her predecessor for the first time on 23 February 2006 at Long Beach, California. (*Cunard*)

Right: The *Queen Elizabeth* passes Lower Manhattan on her final eastbound crossing in October 1968. (*Gillespie-Faber collection*)

rich in harbour oil monies—bought her as a tourist attraction (hotel, museum and collection of shops). She arrived in December 1967, opened in May 1972, and has endured ever since. Indeed, the *Queen Mary* celebrated her seventy-fifth anniversary in 2011.

The *Queen Elizabeth* was far less fortunate. While she might have become a tourist attraction and hotel at Philadelphia, the location changed to Fort Lauderdale, Florida, where she arrived in November 1968. She had seemingly endless financial problems, went bankrupt and then to auction, and was finally bought by Chinese ship-owner C. Y. Tung. *Queen Elizabeth* sailed to Hong Kong to be refitted as the floating university-cruise ship *Seawise University*. Unfortunately, on the eve of returning to service in January 1972, she burned and capsized in Hong Kong harbour. Her remains were later cut up for scrap metal.

Arthur Taylor worked in different aspects of shipping, including marine financing. 'Mainly in the 1960s and 1970s, I was involved in financing by Taiwanese scrap metal companies to buy old ships,' he recalled. 'A twenty-five-year-old, 7,100-ton Liberty ship, for example, changed hands for about $125,000 (in 1970). Some deals failed, of course. I had one Chinese client who wanted to buy the giant *Queen Elizabeth*, which was being auctioned off at Fort Lauderdale in 1970. He wanted it for scrapping. But he didn't have all the monies needed. His plan was to raise money by selling pieces of the ship's two funnels, each a square-inch each and placed in a Plexi-glass block, and then sold all over the world.'

Based in Hong Kong, British-born Taylor did lots of work with many of the great Chinese shipping tycoons, namely C. Y. Tung and Y. K. Pao. 'They bought lots of older second-hand ships as well as brand new ones,' he noted. 'Tung especially was a very interesting man. He began by owning a wheelbarrow and used it along the docks.

Top: *Seawise University* in flames at Hong Kong in January 1972. (*South China Morning Post Ltd*)

Left: Last passage on the mighty Hudson River. (*Richard K. Morse collection*)

In this view from April 1959, the *Mauretania* is headed off on a Caribbean cruise with, from left to right, the *Media, Queen Mary, Ivernia, Liberte, United States* and *Giulio Cesare* in the background. (*Author's collection*)

He was hugely ambitious, worked very hard and soon bought a small tanker. Eventually, he amassed one of the largest fleets in the world, namely the Orient Overseas Line and included ships such as the *Queen Elizabeth, Independence* and *Constitution*. Stories to this day of him sabotaging the former *Queen Elizabeth* aka *Seawise University* in 1972 for insurance reasons are totally unfounded. Indeed, Tung was very proud of buying the famous Cunard liner. Later, when visiting him at his townhouse in London where he had his own cinema, Tung showed films of the *Queen Elizabeth*, his other passenger ships, and even freighters and tankers. As we sat back and watched, he smiled and beamed with pride.'

Chapter Three

LAST OF THE FOUR STACKERS
Aquitania

On the old North Atlantic run, she remained one of the grandest and most palatial liners of all time. Her late Edwardian interiors were sumptuously stunning. Indeed, she was part of that unique group of large liners known as the 'floating palaces'. The grand old *Aquitania* was one of the largest ships of her day and later ranked as the last ocean liner with four funnels. She survived two world wars and sailed for Cunard for thirty-five years until 1949.

Building at the John Brown shipyard in Scotland when the *Titanic* sank on the freezing Atlantic in April of 1912, the *Aquitania* was completed in the spring of 1914. Soon after her maiden voyage, she went into grey-painted war duties and later served as a hospital ship. In the 1920s and 1930s, the *Aquitania* was one of Cunard's great express liners—the 'Big Three' that also included the first *Mauretania* and *Berengaria*. It was six days from New York to Cherbourg and Southampton. By 1938, when she was sailing alongside the brand new *Queen Mary,* her first-class fares started at $219, tourist class at $130 and third class at $85. That same year, Lewis and Ruth Gordon sailed on the first of almost 100 crossings to and from Europe. 'We went over on the *Aquitania* and then came home on the *Berengaria*. We travelled third class and so we were "locked out" of first and even tourist class. But one evening, I found the fire stairs that led into first class. I remember seeing great cheeses on the bar tops and the beef being carved at dining room tables.'

The 45,647-ton *Aquitania* carried as many as 3,230 passengers: 618 in first class, 614 in tourist and 1,998 in third. 'There wasn't any running water in third-class cabins then,' recalled Lewis Gordon. 'A container called a Levebo, which was ceramic and round, had a little spigot from which water was poured. Each day, it was refilled by the steward. There were no private bathrooms either. You made an appointment with a special bath steward for the use of a little room that contained a tub and a chair. You were allowed thirty minutes. He would knock on your cabin door and announce when your bath was ready—and also knock when your time had ended.'

While the 901-foot-long *Aquitania* might have gone to the scrapyard in 1940, just as the new *Queen Elizabeth* was to come into service, she endured to serve in another world war. She travelled all over the world—to Sydney, Singapore, Cape Town and San Francisco. Afterwards in the late 1940s, when the *Aquitania* resumed transatlantic service, she was not quite her gracious self.

Instead, she was used on a one-class austerity service that was run by Cunard, but subsidised by the Canadian Government and carried mostly immigrants, troops and their families between Southampton and Halifax. However, by December 1949, she had grown old, tired and was no longer able to safely withstand another treacherous Atlantic winter. As a consequence, the British Board of Trade refused to renew her sailing permit. And so after thirty-five years, 443 sailings, 3,000,000 miles and 1,200,000 passengers, the *Aquitania* was sold to shipbreakers at Faslane in Scotland; however, bits and pieces from her lived on for some years afterwards. Her carpets, for example, were placed on the *Britannic* that sailed until 1960. Also, her first-class restaurant chairs found their way aboard the *Carinthia*, which sailed for Cunard from 1956 until 1967.

Late August 1939 and the *Normandie*, *Aquitania* and *Roma* of the Italian Line are in port. (*Port Authority of New York & New Jersey*)

The *Aquitania* arrives from Southampton, already in grey war colouring in this view dated September 1939. The *Normandie* is on the left; the *Queen Mary* on the right. (*Cronican-Arroyo collection*)

The last four-stacker: the stately *Aquitania*, still in war colours, arrives at Pier 90 in this view from 1945. (*Cronican-Arroyo collection*)

Chapter Four

PRE-WAR INTERMEDIATES
Scythia, Samaria, Franconia and Ascania

Cunard lost many of their passenger ships during the Second World War, some in enemy action and others to the British Government that converted them into full-time military ships. Some even remained in Government service until as late as the 1960s. Of the fleet of moderately-sized, single-stack passenger ships the company created in the 1920s, only four were suitable for further commercial service after 1945. There were the 20,000-ton sisters and near-sisters *Franconia, Samaria* and *Scythia,* and one smaller ship, the 14,000-ton *Ascania*. They were each refurbished in the late 1940s, specifically to revive Cunard services to Canada—Quebec City in the ice-free months on the St Lawrence (from April through December) and then alternately to Halifax and New York for the remainder.

The 623-foot-long *Franconia* was perhaps the most famous. Richard Gibson, who was the hygiene officer onboard the *QE2* in the mid-1980s, joined Cunard during the war in 1943. His very first ship was the troopship *Franconia*. 'When I joined her, she was carrying troops out to Sicily. My first trip was with forty-two other converted passenger ships as well as freighters, most of them headed for Algiers,' he recalled. 'I started as a deck boy and received five dollars per month and forty dollars danger money. We had 300 troops onboard. The port engines had been damaged and so we had to make do with only one engine, making a mere 10-11 knots, but which was adequate for the 8-knot speed of our convoy. After we delivered our troops to Algiers and then continued on to Malta, we returned to the UK, but with only one escorting warship. Usually,

there were more. The *Franconia* was then laid up for four-and-a-half months of repairs off Gareloch Head in Scotland. Afterwards, we began trooping on the North Atlantic to Halifax and New York.'

By the end of the war in 1944–45, Houghton was serving in a former White Star liner, the greatly rebuilt *Georgic* that had been bombed in 1941 and then endured a long and tedious rebuilding. Soon after, he was assigned to the *Franconia* and just in time for the famed Yalta conference. 'The ship was used as Winston Churchill's headquarters,' he noted. 'He lived and worked from a refurbished suite onboard. I especially remember him spending long hours soaking in the tub and where he wrote and read from a special-ly-built shelf that rested across the top of the tub. The steward's bell was, however, at the far end of the tub. Therefore, when the Prime Minister wanted more hot water, he would ring by simply using his big toe. Also, he spent long stretches in the confines of his suite working in the nude. Apparently, he often dictated to aids in this manner as well. I also recall disembarking from the *Queen Mary* in Cowes Roads in a special torpedo boat. The troops, anxious to get ashore, were not pleased with even the slightest delay. There was, as I remember, some unpleasant yelling. Churchill, on the other hand, simply responded with an aristocratic wave.'

Beginning in the late 1940s, these four old Cunarders were restored and used mostly in the Canadian trade from London, Liverpool and Southampton. Occasionally, they appeared on the run to New York as well and each ship was scrapped by the late 1950s.

The 20,000-grt *Samaria* was one of four older Cunarders, all dating from the 1920s, which were used well into the 1950s. (*Cunard*)

The *Britannic* visiting Boston in the late 1930s. (*ALF collection*)

Chapter Five

LAST OF WHITE STAR LINE
Britannic

'The *Britannic* had some of the most beautiful public rooms of any of our ships in the 1950s,' recalled John Ferguson, then a staff member at Cunard Line's offices in Broadway, New York. 'There were exquisite and perfectly polished woods. There were columned lounges with big sofas and enormous soft chairs. There were fireplaces, crystal ceiling lamps and magnificent carpets, some of which came from the great *Aquitania* from before the war. A very popular and sturdy ship, she ran Cunard's then busy service between New York, Cobh and Liverpool. She was a great favourite to many travellers in those final boom years on the North Atlantic.'

Built by the famed Harland and Wolff shipyard at Belfast, the 712-foot-long *Britannic* was commissioned in 1930. But even her inaugural sparkle and brightness were somewhat dimmed by the dark and gathering clouds of the Great Depression. Like so many other passenger ships, the *Britannic* would struggle to fill her berths in the ensuing years. In sleek Art Deco Moderne, she was an especially long and low-looking ship with two squat stacks (only the second worked; the front stack was the wireless room), a slightly raked bow and a classic cruiser stern. Danish-built Burmeister & Wain diesels made her one of the largest motor liners of her time. The original passenger berths totalled 1,553 in three classes and there was room for cargo in no less than seven holds. Transatlantic crossings were spaced with periodic Caribbean and Mediterranean cruises. She also ran a number of short 'get away' trips such as three-day weekend cruises up to Halifax from New York as well

as six and seven night jaunts to Bermuda or Nassau. Fares for a three-day long weekend cruise in the mid-1930s started at forty-five dollars. However, the 19-knot ship was called to more urgent duty just after the Second World War began in September 1939. The *Britannic* was painted over entirely in sombre greys and spent the next six years as a troop transport.

She rejoined Cunard-White Star (the double title would be used until 1950) in 1948, but still sported her original White Star colours of buff and black on her funnels. The Cunard colours of black top and orange-red with two black stripes would not have worked on such squat-sized stacks. Fully refurbished, her quarters were restyled for two classes in the post-war era: 429 in first class and 569 in tourist. An annual nine-week Mediterranean-Black Sea cruise, which departed from New York each January, was a highlight of her schedules. Ports of call for the 1960 cruise included the likes of Madeira, Gibraltar, Villefranche, Naples, Mykonos, Haifa, Istanbul and Odessa.

Prompted by increasing old age, the *Britannic* had a massive mechanical breakdown, a broken crankshaft, in the spring of 1960 and had to remain along the south side of New York's Pier 90 for months while undergoing repairs. Using barges as floating workshops, it then ranked as the largest pier-side repair job of its kind. Todd Shipyards did the work, based out of their plant over in Red Hook, Brooklyn; however, it cost Cunard millions, including lost bookings and cancellations. The thirty-year-old ship's fate was sealed.

She was the first of the post-war fleet of large liners to go, those twelve passenger ships that by 1957 made Cunard the largest and busiest on the North Atlantic. By 1960, the airlines were cutting deeply into Cunard's share of that trans-ocean trade.

And so, on a moody December afternoon in 1960, the *Britannic*—the last of the White Star liners—sailed from New York for the final time. After de-storing at Liverpool, she headed north to Inverkeitking in Scotland to be scrapped. The *Britannic*'s career was finished lasting from 1930 to 1960.

Top: The flag-bedecked *Britannic* anchored at Istanbul during a long winter Mediterranean cruise in 1955. (*ALF collection*)

Above: The *Queen Mary* gets underway on a Wednesday afternoon sailing as the *Britannic* remains in port until Friday. (*ALF collection*)

Right: A lavish 1930s brochure for *Britannic* cruises. (*Andrew Kilk collection*)

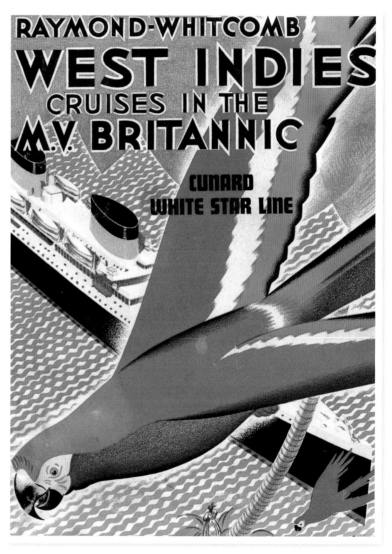

Outbound from New York on a sixty-day winter Mediterranean cruise, the brilliant *Britannic*, as Cunard dubbed her, passes Battery Park at the lower end of Manhattan. (*Cronican-Arroyo collection*)

Chapter Six

AUSTERITY AND LOW FARES
Georgic

On the *Georgic*, which was never fully repaired after war damage in 1941 and was Cunard's least popular passenger ship in the 1950s, life was perhaps hardest of all. She sailed the low fare, all tourist-class runs between Southampton or Liverpool, Le Havre, Cobh, Halifax and New York in peak summer and then carried British immigrants to Australia for most of the remainder. 'Cunard could not get a regular company crew to man her and so went round to the jails and prisons at Southampton and Liverpool and gathered up those willing to sail and serve as waiters and stewards. But it never really worked,' remembered a former ship's engineer. 'They were the roughest lot. There was endless fighting onboard and then, when ashore, they fought in waterfront bars and pubs and often wrecked them. They were also very lazy and often paid the immigrant passengers to do their jobs. As they often slept in pantries, closets and linen lockers, some passengers in the lower deck quarters were cleaning cabins, making beds, washing out lavatories and public showers, and mopping the lino-covered floors.'

The *Georgic* had a diverse career. 'By the end of the Second World War, I was serving aboard the largely rebuilt *Georgic*, the former White Star liner that that had been bombed and set afire in Egypt in 1941. She later endured a tedious salvage, a long and slow tow back to the UK, and then very extended repairs and rebuilding,' recalled Len Houghton. 'But even after her reconstruction (at Harland and Wolff at Belfast), some of her beams and other parts were still twisted and mangled. The damages were still quite evident. The crew nicknamed her the "corrugated lung".'

Between 1950 and 1955 when there was tremendous demand for accommodation on the Atlantic run, Cunard chartered the *Georgic* for peak summer season service between Southampton or Liverpool, Le Havre, Cobh, Halifax and New York. Her capacity was listed as 1,962 in low fare tourist class. 'We had immigrants going westbound and budget tourists in reverse,' added Houghton. 'The facilities onboard were very basic, even below our normal tourist-class standard. The ship's restaurant, for example, was like a big cafeteria. Everyone carried trays during meals. Her general condition was such, however, that the London surveyors would not let her sail the North Atlantic in winter. Instead, she reverted to the Ministry of Transport and sailed on the Australian migrant run, sailing to Fremantle, Melbourne and Sydney via the Suez or on Government trooping.'

The 711-foot-long *Georgic* finished her final Cunard transatlantic charter in October 1955 and then, after one more winter on the Australian run, she went to the breakers at Faslane in Scotland.

Opposite: Reduced to a single funnel, the austerity-style *Georgic* passes through the Panama Canal in this view dated 9 June 1949, returning from Australia to Southampton. (*Cronican-Arroyo collection*)

Chapter Seven

THE 'NEW' MAURETANIA

Captain Robin Woodall, who joined Cunard in 1950 and retired in 1994 as commodore aboard the mighty *QE2*, fondly remembered the ship that was often known as the 'new' *Mauretania*. He served aboard the 772-foot-long ship in the early 1960s just as the grand era of transatlantic passenger shipping was drawing to a close. 'Immediately after the first commercial jet flight between London and New York in October 1958, steamship lines began to lose clientele,' he said. 'Cunard, with no less than a dozen liners in Atlantic service to New York and to Canada, was no exception. All of our ships began to suffer—and suffer quickly. I remember being aboard the *Mauretania* and with the ship having more crew than passengers. By 1961, she actually had to skip some scheduled sailings simply because there weren't enough passengers.'

When the Second World War dramatically erupted in the late summer of 1939, Lee Houghton's travels on Cunard expanded. 'In August 1939, I was in the *Samaria* just as she was hurriedly painted over in grey and began to sail in blackout. Soon afterwards in the following spring, I joined the brand new *Mauretania*. I went out on her first wartime trooping voyage from New York to Australia via the Panama Canal, San Francisco and Honolulu. When we docked at Sydney's Circular Quay, we caused great excitement. At over 35,000 tons, we were one of the biggest liners yet seen in those far-off waters. The Australians had never expected to see one of the big North Atlantic ocean liners. However, when the *Queen Mary* arrived shortly thereafter in May 1940, we were completely and utterly pre-empted. The giant, grey-painted *Mary* had to anchor off Woolloomooloo Steps. She was, of course, far too large to berth alongside in a port like Sydney.'

A handsome-looking ship that appeared to be a first cousin to the larger *Queen Elizabeth*, the *Mauretania* was designed by naval architects who had worked on a number of P&O liners during the early 1930s. Consequently, the *Mauretania* bore a resemblance to the otherwise single-funnelled *Stratheden*. The *Mauretania* also had an inviting, warm, almost club-like feel to some of her interiors. Some passengers, including Hollywood actress Lana Turner preferred the *Mauretania* over the large hotel atmosphere of the *Queens*. After the war, the *Mauretania* could carry a total of 1,140 passengers—470 in first class, 370 in cabin class and 300 in tourist.

The 23-knot ship sailed for about nine months of the year, April through November, between New York, Cobh, Le Havre and Southampton. The rest of the time, she went cruising from New York to the Caribbean. Usually on two and three-week itineraries, her ports of call included the likes of Havana, Port-au-Prince, Kingston and Cristobal. Minimum fare for a two-week cruise in 1960 was four hundred dollars.

'Having crossed on both the *Queen Mary* and the *Queen Elizabeth*, I preferred the somewhat smaller *Mauretania*,' noted the late Everett Viez, a world-class ocean liner collector and frequent trans-ocean as well as cruise passenger. 'The *Mauretania* was somewhat smaller and therefore warmer and perhaps cosier than the two big *Queens*.

Top: Maiden arrival of the 'new' *Mauretania* at New York in June 1939. (*Cunard*)

Above: The *Empress of Japan* and *Mauretania* at Wellington in 1940. (*ALF collection*)

Right: The *Mauretania* berthed at New York in a view dated 7 April 1958. (*Author's collection*)

Twilight years: Painted in cruising green, the *Mauretania* is seen here on the north side of Pier 92, New York in 1964. She would be retired in the following year. (*ALF Collection*)

This was an attraction. She was actually very much of a mini version of the *Queen Elizabeth*. But, of course, the *Mauretania* was slower and therefore took an extra day to Southampton—six days in all from New York. Many passengers including myself preferred this. The five-day crossings on the *Queens* were in ways almost hurried, more like a long weekend at sea, say, Thursday to Monday on the westbound crossings. It seemed you were arriving at Pier 90 before you knew it!'

As something of a last ditch effort to secure added passengers, Cunard decided—in what proved to be a misguided decision—to place the now all-green *Mauretania* in Mediterranean service. Routed between Naples, Genoa, Cannes, Gibraltar and New York, it was hoped that she would successfully compete with the likes of the American Export and Italian liners on the same run. Instead, she was a complete flop, losing further money for her struggling Liverpool-based owners. With the *Britannic, Media* and *Parthia* already gone, the *Mauretania* seemed to be next.

Left: The 772-foot-long *Mauretania* in her 'cruising green' at New York in 1963 with the *Queen Elizabeth* on the other side of Pier 90. (*Richard Turnwald collection*)

Right: Winter Sunshine Cruises. (*Andrew Kilk collection*)

The very handsome *Mauretania* at New York. (*ALF collection*)

The *Mauretania* returns from the sunny Caribbean to a very cold and icy New York in this scene dated February 1959. (*Richard Faber collection*)

Outbound for the warm Caribbean, the 23-knot *Mauretania* heads off on a fourteen-night cruise. (*Richard Turnwald collection*)

The Chrysler Building looms over the *Mauretania* in this early 1960s view. Just to the left, the Pan Am Building is under construction. (*Richard Weiss collection*)

The *Mauretania* was often compared as being a 'baby version' of the *Queen Elizabeth*. (*Gillespie-Faber collection*)

David Gibson worked for Cunard for some fifty years. He recalled, 'In the early 1960s, everything was beginning to change. The jets were intruding on the Atlantic and Cunard was retreating in decline. There were fewer and fewer passengers on the crossings. I was posted to the *Mauretania*, which was struggling and had been transferred to a new Mediterranean-New York service. This was, of course, a great mistake. Both the Italian Line and American Export Lines dominated that passenger service. On the *Mauretania*, I was a first-class assistant purser, which had to be the easiest job at sea. I remember crossings with only thirty passengers in first class and another trip with seventeen (out of 400 beds) and altogether having only 200 or 300 passengers on a ship that otherwise could carry 1,200. The *Mauretania* seemed like a "ghost ship". I also sailed on the *Queen Elizabeth* and on the *Caronia*, on one of her six-week summer cruises from New York to Norway. The *Caronia* was kept "alive" by bunches of old, rich ladies that lived aboard for months and sometimes years at a time. I left Cunard in 1965, just before the

big crunch and more serious cuts. But I treasure the experience of those times with Cunard. It was the end of a golden age, a bygone era and it was exciting to be a part of that.'

'By 1965, the last *Mauretania* cruises were actual charters to the Ford Motor Company,' added John Ferguson. 'They were special incentives between New York and Lisbon, one way by sea and the other by air. I remember a young executive named Lee Iacocca being aboard (an American businessman known for designing the iconic Ford Mustang). The very last *Mauretania* cruise, a two-month Mediterranean-Black Sea itinerary that left New York and ended at Southampton, actually had very few passengers. They were the last guests to come down her gangways.'

While her Cunard owners perhaps might have hoped for a more profitable resale, possibly for further service, only scrap metal dealers in Scotland at Inverkeithing were interested. Stripped of her finery, the once grand *Mauretania* was retired in November 1965 and then gone within six months.

The *Queen Mary* and green-coloured *Mauretania* meet at the Ocean Dock, Southampton, in 1963. (*Cunard*)

Chapter Eight

GREEN GODDESS
Luxurious Caronia

The *Caronia* was the first purpose-built liner after the war to capture the lucrative American cruise market, air-conditioned throughout and for rich Americans to cruise around the world. Brenton Jenkins recalled: 'Ralph Newcombe was the staff purser of the *Queen Mary* at the time and was appointed to be the chief purser of the brand new *Caronia*. He took with him from the first-class purser's office of the *Queen Mary*: Colin Bellamy as his staff purser, Elizabeth Sayers as his senior lady assistant purser and me to be his second assistant purser. All of us worked in the first-class office. The *Caronia* had a cabin class, but only for transatlantic voyages and never on any cruises. She was all first class on cruises.'

'The *Caronia* was a very elegant ship. She was the premier luxury cruise ship of the 1950s and one of the very finest Cunard liners of all time,' according to Lewis Gordon who made two trips in her—an Atlantic crossing and a six-week summer cruise from New York to Scandinavia. 'On that cruise, like all *Caronia* cruises, the passengers were very wealthy,' he added.

Built at the John Brown shipyard at Clydebank and commissioned in December 1948, the 34,100-ton *Caronia* was a predecessor to today's six-star-rated cruise ships—to the likes of Crystal Cruises, Oceania, Silversea, Seabourn, Regent and Seadream. She had an enviable exclusivity about her. Other companies tried to copy from her, even duplicate her. Painted overall in several shades of green and known everywhere as the 'Green Goddess', she had 600 hand-picked crewmembers to look after her 600 cruise passengers. (Her capacity was 932, officially divided between 581 in first class and 351 in cabin class.)

Mostly, however, she carried about 350. Cunard accountants were far more tolerant than the directors who were more interested in prestige and status. She was often likened to a huge floating country club. She ran similar cruises year after year and around the world such as Africa, circling the Pacific, Mediterranean and the North Cape. The *Caronia* inspired such passenger loyalty that some guests lived aboard for months, sometimes years at a time. Another, and an all-time record breaker, stayed for an incredible fourteen years.

Len Houghton was posted to the extraordinary *Caronia* for eight years. 'Her long, expensive, near-continual cruises lured a special clientele,' he recalled. 'We had women onboard like Miss Smith and Miss Jones who joined the ninety-five day world cruise in January, then the six-week 'Meddy' (Mediterranean) and then finished with the forty-five night summer North Cape cruise. When we reached Southampton, they went up to London, to the Dorchester or the Savoy, spent several weeks there and then crossed homeward on one of the *Queens*.'

Opposite above: The splendid, 34,000-grt *Caronia* was Britain's biggest post-war liner, seen here on her speed trial in the fall of 1948. (*Luis Miguel Correia Collection*)

Opposite below: The *Caronia* at Auckland in February 1951. (*Author's collection*)

Clockwise from top left:
Maiden arrival at New York in
January 1949. (*Moran Towing &
Transportation Co.*)

The *Caronia* waits to sail on
another long and luxurious
cruise. (*Richard Turnwald
collection*)

The cabin-class main lounge.
(*Author's collection*)

The first-class main restaurant. (*Author's collection*)

'On her North Cape fjords cruise, we sailed from New York on 1 July,' recalled Lewis Gordon. 'Sailing day was like a great big reunion—there were so many repeaters and everyone knew one another from years of travel together. Then once underway, these people threw very elaborate theme parties and invited hundreds of their fellow passengers. They paid for all the drinks, but in those days, Cunard provided all the refreshments. Being invited to one of these gala events was a chance for us to mingle with the millionaire set. The service onboard the *Caronia* was absolutely magnificent. Anything you wanted you could have. Your clothes were always laid out and your shoes freshly polished. Of course, we dressed every night except Sunday. The restaurants—the Balmoral and the Sandringham—were *à la carte*. Special dinner requests were made at lunch and then items prepared for dinner. In our fifty-eight years of ocean travel, the *Caronia* still ranked as having the very best food. My favourite was *Salmon a la Russe*, which is smoked salmon overlaid with caviar.

'Most *Caronia* cruises finished at Southampton, but the cruise fare always included a first-class return to New York in any Cunarder within a year. This included either the *Queen Mary* or the *Queen Elizabeth*. Most passengers preferred it this way.

WRITING ROOM R.mS. CARONIA.

The writing room onboard *Caronia*. (*Author's collection*)

After our North Cape cruise, most passengers went to European spas, to Baden-Baden and Montecatini mostly, and then would return to New York in September on the *Caronia* or one of the *Queens*. We were booked on the *Caronia* after our summer cruise on a Southampton-Le Havre-New York crossing and so had deliberately left much of our clothing onboard. But we were delayed on the train coming down from London to Southampton and finally

arrived just in time to see her sail off. A Cunard official on the pier side saved the day, however. He found a cabin for us on the nearby *Queen Mary* that was sailing two hours later. It was a most convenient alternative. We reached New York in five days, a full two days ahead of the *Caronia*. Somewhere in the North Atlantic, we passed that ship and our clothing. At New York, we disembarked from the *Queen Mary* and cleared immigration and customs. Two days later, I had to return to Pier 90, collect our luggage from the *Caronia*, and then clear immigration and customs for a second time.'

During Cunard's massive fleet reduction in the late 1960s, the *Caronia* was decommissioned in October 1967. She was later sold to Greek buyers, renamed *Caribia*, and was intended to run New York-Caribbean cruises. She resumed service, had a fire in the Caribbean and later returned to New York only to slip into an idle and neglected state. Laid up for her remaining years, she was finally sold to Taiwanese scrappers in 1974, but then wrecked while en route and under tow in a ferocious storm near Guam that August. She broke in three after crashing into a local breakwater and her remains were later removed and demolished.

Left: A first-class deck plan. (*Andrew Kilk collection*)

Right: The great world cruise of 1964. (*Andrew Kilk collection*)

Overleaf: Bon voyage to the *Caronia* at New York. (*Cunard*)

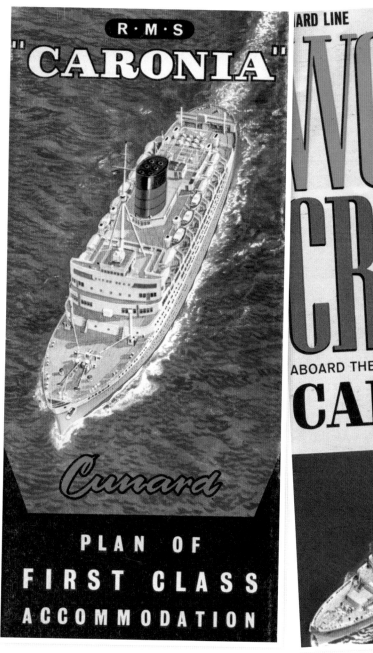

Chapter Nine

COMBINATION SHIPS
Media and Parthia

'In the 1950s, we sailed very often on the Cunard Line. It was our favourite company then for our trips across the Atlantic. We always thought the two *Queens*, the old *Elizabeth* and *Mary*, were too big, too much like hotels and so we preferred smaller ships,' recalled Jack Allyn. He and his family made over twenty crossings with Cunard in those years. 'We sailed on the *Scythia* and the *Ascania*, which were quite elderly and creaking even then. Later, we crossed on the newer *Sylvania* and *Carinthia*. But our great favourites were the sisters *Media* and *Parthia*. We made six crossings on those ships. They carried only 250 passengers each, all in first class, but it was often as few as seventy-five or 100 fellow travellers. On one November crossing, we only had twenty-six passengers onboard the *Parthia*. And so, we called them the "Cunard yachts".'

Just as the Second World War ended, Cunard decided to build three new passenger ships to reinforce and replenish its fleet—the impressive 34,000-ton *Caronia*, the world's first full-time cruise ship, and two combination passenger-cargo ships. These were the 13,300-ton *Media* and *Parthia*, and they were especially created for the Liverpool-New York direct service. Actually, the initial plan was for twelve-passenger freighters for the Port Line, a Cunard subsidiary. They would have sailed in far different waters from British ports out to Australia and New Zealand with large cargoes of meat on the return voyages. However, they were moved over to Cunard's order book in the rethinking of 1945–46. Both came from distinguished builders—the *Media* from the John Brown shipyard at Clydebank

in Scotland and where the *Queen Mary*, *Queen Elizabeth* and subsequent *QE2* were created; the *Parthia* was from Harland and Wolff at Belfast, builders of the immortal *Titanic*.

The 531-foot-long *Media* appeared first in the summer of 1947 and became the first brand new passenger ship to come on the Atlantic run since the war had ended. Once the *Parthia* entered service in April 1948, one of the pair came and went every other week, arriving in New York on Saturday and then sailing home to England on the following Friday. They tended to use the north side of Cunard's Pier 92 at the foot of West 52nd Street. Pier 90 was generally reserved for the *Queens* and other large liners. Today, the north side of Pier 92 is Berth 6, part of New York City's consolidated three-pier cruise terminal. Periodically, the itineraries of the *Media* and *Parthia* were altered slightly to include special calls at Greenock, Cobh, Norfolk and Bermuda.

Robert Welding was first assigned to the Cunard sisters *Media* and *Parthia*. 'We had long stays in port at each end in those days,' recalled Welding. 'We'd arrive in New York on a Saturday and then not sail again until the following Friday. That was six days in port and lots of ashore time for the crew. They were gorgeous little ships, beautifully decorated, like miniature versions of first class on the big *Queen Mary* and *Queen Elizabeth*. We had lots of top business people onboard, passengers who preferred more leisurely crossings and the occasional celebrity such as Katharine Hepburn.

'My grandfather was with the White Star Line, sailing on the *Olympic*—sister of the *Titanic*—*Homeric* and *Majestic*. My father

Above: The handsome combination passenger-cargo liner *Media* was the first Cunarder to have stabilisers. They were fitted in 1952. (*Author's collection*)

Below left: The 13,500-grt *Media* loading cargo at Liverpool. (*ALF collection*)

Below right: Saturday afternoon and the *Parthia* arrives at New York. (*Philippe Brebant collection*)

The main lounge aboard the *Parthia*. (*Richard Faber collection*)

followed but with Cunard–White Star in the late 1930s, working aboard the *Berengaria*, *Britannic*, *Georgic* and one voyage on the brand new *Queen Mary*. He started as a bellman making fifteen dollars a month. I joined Cunard out of Liverpool in the 1950s, crossing mostly on the *Media* and *Parthia*, smaller combo passenger-cargo ships that carried about 250 passengers each and all of them in first class. Those ships were like yachts: slow and leisurely, like woody clubs on the inside. We had lots of select passengers on those nine-night crossings to and from New York. I remember Katharine Hepburn being aboard, some West End actors and actresses, and

several important ministers from London. Things were up by then, of course. I was making as much as forty to fifty dollars a month!'

Len Houghton was also posted to the *Media* and *Parthia* in the 1950s. 'They were very smart little ships with equivalent all-first-class accommodations,' he remembered. 'But cargo was a big part of their operation. We often carried thoroughbreds from Cobh in Ireland to New York where they were all trans-shipped to Kentucky. One officer onboard the *Media* used to log all the manure just for his garden

The lounge aboard the *Media*. (*Albert Wilhelmi collection*)

back home. We also carried lots of grain to the UK and sometimes we would make a short detour to Norfolk and load tobacco.'

The *Media* and *Parthia* had comparatively short careers with Cunard. Within ten years by the late 1950s, they had grown increasingly unprofitable. They often missed taking on valuable cargoes due to their strict passenger schedules. In 1961 and the beginning of the dismantling of the great Cunard Atlantic fleet, they were withdrawn and sold—the *Media* to the Italian Cogedar Line and *Parthia* to another British passenger ship firm, the New Zealand Shipping Company. The *Media* was gutted and totally made over as the 1,320-passenger *Flavia* for the Europe–Australia immigrant and low-fare tourist trades. She joined another Italian company, the Costa Line, in 1968 and thereafter sailed mostly on Miami–Nassau–Freeport cruise services until sold to Hong Kong and Chinese buyers in 1982. While being refitted, she burned out and capsized in Hong Kong harbour in January 1989 before being scrapped. The *Parthia* sailed for a few years between England and New Zealand via the Panama Canal as the *Remuera* and later became the *Aramac*. She sailed for a division of P&O, the Sydney-headquartered Eastern & Australian Lines, in a triangular service between Australia, Hong Kong and Japan. She finished up in the hands of Taiwanese shipbreakers in 1970.

Chapter Ten

ON CHARTER
P&O's Stratheden

During the boom summer season of 1950 as Atlantic travel was fully reawakening, Cunard chartered one of P&O Lines' largest passenger liners: the 23,700-ton *Stratheden*. A rather glorious looking white-hulled ship that could carry up to 980 passengers—527 in first class and 453 in tourist—she was needed to assist the 'overbooked' *Queen Elizabeth*, *Queen Mary* and *Mauretania* on the express run. The *Stratheden* made four roundtrips between Southampton, Le Havre, Halifax and New York.

The 20-knot *Stratheden* had been built in 1937 at the Vickers-Armstrong yard at Barrow-in-Furness and sailed during the war as a troopship. Other than Cunard crossings and occasional cruises for P&O, she was used in the mainline Australian service, sailing from London to Gibraltar, Aden, Bombay, Colombo, Adelaide, Fremantle, Melbourne and Sydney. On the return, there were calls at Marseilles, a port where many passengers left the ship, and took trains across France and then to the UK to save time as well as avoiding the infamous Bay of Biscay. Like all large P&O liners of the time, the *Stratheden* had a considerable cargo capacity in six holds.

The 665-foot-long *Stratheden* sailed for P&O until 1964 when she was sold to Greek interests: the Latsis Line. She became the *Henrietta Latsi* and later *Marianna Latsi*, mostly for Muslim religious pilgrim voyages between North and West African ports, and Jeddah in Saudi Arabia. She was finally scrapped in Italy in 1969.

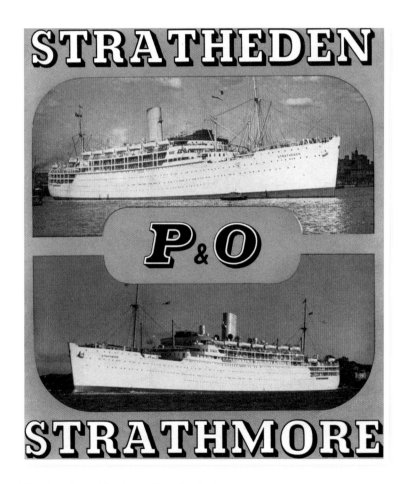

P&O brochure. (*Andrew Kilk collection*)

On charter from P&O: the 23,000-grt *Stratheden* made four trips to New York in 1950. (*Albert Wilhelmi collection*)

Chapter Eleven

LAST ATLANTIC CUNARDERS

Saxonia/Carmania, Ivernia/Franconia, Carinthia and Sylvania

Ports in the Mediterranean, especially in the east, used to feature a veritable wealth of passenger ships. Some were larger and well known while others were smaller and less familiar; however, this made them even more curious and intriguing. Other ships had been rebuilt and changed beyond recognition. The author recalls seeing former Soviet passenger ships, ex-Japanese railway carriers and second and third generation Scandinavian ferries. In the summer of 1993, at Naples and then at Valletta on Malta, the author came across two once familiar passenger liners: the onetime Cunarders *Saxonia* (later *Carmania*) and *Ivernia* (later *Franconia*). They were then the Ukrainian-owned *Leonid Sobinov* and *Feodor Shalyapin*.

Nearly forty years old at the time, the two ships were built for the last heyday of the Atlantic liner trade. Cunard still reigned supreme in that service and in 1954, added the first of four identical sister ships for their run to Eastern Canada, Quebec City and Montreal. From December through April and when the St Lawrence River was clogged in ice, they sailed to Halifax and New York. Along with their Atlantic crossings, the two-day trips between Nova Scotia port and New York were offered at twenty-five dollars per person in tourist class.

Built in Scotland at the same John Brown shipyard where the *Queen Mary*, *Queen Elizabeth*, *Caronia* and *QE2* were built, the *Saxonia* was launched by Lady Churchill in February 1954. She and the *Ivernia* were teamed on the run from London, Le Havre and Southampton; the subsequent *Carinthia* and *Sylvania* operated out of Liverpool and Greenock. At over 22,000 tons each and with capacities for some 900 passengers in two classes, they were also designed to carry lots of cargo—six holds in all. The trade began to change soon after they were all delivered by 1957, however. The airlines soon began to take their passengers and freight.

'It was most unfortunate that these ships were not designed with a stronger consideration toward cruising. This would have saved them in the Cunard fleet,' states Captain Robin Woodall. 'They were Cunard's last purposeful Atlantic liners, ships that were sadly unsuccessful almost from the start. Basically, they were indoor ships. They lacked outdoor pools and sun decks, for example, and had far too few cabins with private bathroom facilities, which American cruise passengers much preferred.'

Cunard did rethink their practices for at least two of these ships. In extended refits in 1962–63, which included experimentation and testing for the projected new Atlantic superliner that would become the *QE2*, the *Saxonia* and *Ivernia* were rebuilt for half-year cruising in the sun. In the image of the glorious *Caronia*, they were repainted in all green. Their aft cargo spaces were gone, replaced with an umbrella-lined lido deck (an Italian word for a beach) and oval-shaped swimming pool. All of their cabins were fitted with private bathrooms. Their crossings were extended for extra business to include Rotterdam in Holland. Soon, they would abandon their Atlantic crossings altogether and run cruises for twelve months of the year.

Clockwise from top left:

The 23,000-grt *Sylvania* fitting at John Brown's shipyard at Clydebank in 1957. (*Cunard*)

The *Saxonia* and her sisters were easily recognisable by their domed funnels. (*Cunard*)

The *Sylvania* and her sisters would often spend six days in New York, mostly for cargo handling. (*ALF collection*)

On a winter's Friday morning, the 19-knot *Saxonia* departs for Halifax, Cobh, Southampton, Le Havre and London. (*ALF collection*)

The *Carinthia* arriving at Montreal for the first time. (*Cunard*)

The drawing room and library aboard the *Saxonia* completed in 1954. (*Author's collection*)

Left: The *Saxonia* remains at dock as the *Sylvania* departs. (*Gillespie-Faber collection*)

Right: About to be modernised and restyled as part-time cruise ships, the *Saxonia* and *Ivernia* returned to John Brown's shipyard in 1962. They would reappear as the *Carmania* and *Franconia*. (*Cunard*)

The *Saxonia*, as the renamed *Carmania*, cruised from Port Everglades, Florida, in winter and for the remainder from Southampton to the Mediterranean, West Africa, the Atlantic Isles and Scandinavia. The *Ivernia*, as the *Franconia*, took over the seasonal New York-Bermuda cruise run vacated by the Furness-Bermuda Line's *Queen of Bermuda* and *Ocean Monarch* in 1966. Both ships remained in what would become an increasingly shrunken Cunard passenger fleet until 1971. By then, they were victims of soaring operational costs, demanding British seamen's unions and flashy and new foreign flag competitors. After the inaugural of the *QE2* in 1969, these two Cunard fleet-mates fell out of step and favour, especially with an increasingly ruthless generation of home office accountants. Both ships were ageing and in need of upgrading and modernisation. In the autumn of 1971, they were laid up in the River Fall in Cornwall, England, and offered for sale.

Initially, the Japanese wanted them for Pacific Ocean cruising and then Greece's Chandris Lines thought of rebuilding them for their Europe-Australia and around the world passenger trades. Instead, the Soviets bought them (in 1973 and after a two-year lay-up) through a Liberian-flag intermediary for their Odessa-based Black Sea Shipping Company.

'Ted Arison had a look over the *Carmania* and *Franconia* in late 1971,' recalled the late Arthur Crook, a British ship designer and surveyor. 'He had come over from Miami and travelled down to Cornwall to see the otherwise dark and silent ships. But Cunard management was suspicious and unsure of him, and would not even turn on some onboard lighting. Arison wanted one of the ships and perhaps might even have bought both, but Cunard refused to negotiate. Instead, Arison left disappointed and then travelled to London where he looked over the laid up *Empress of Canada* at Tilbury Docks. Canadian Pacific was somewhat more trusting and a deal was made, and the ship would eventually become the *Mardi Gras*. She was the very first ship in Arison's new venture: Carnival Cruise Lines. Either the *Carmania*, *Franconia* or both might have been the first ships for the Miami-based cruise giant that now owns the entire Cunard Company (since 1998).'

As the renamed *Leonid Sobinov* and *Feodor Shalyapin*, the Soviets used the pair on a variety of so called 'internal services'—student exchange voyages to Cuba, cultural and industrial displays in the Far East, and some trooping to Africa and the Middle East. Mostly,

Above: The *Franconia* berthed along Front Street at Hamilton in Bermuda. (*ALF collection*)

Left: Tourist class to Canada on the *Saxonia*, *Ivernia* and *Carinthia* in 1961. The *Sylvania*, the fourth sister, had been shifted to the Liverpool-New York run. (*Andrew Kilk collection*)

however, they sailed on Western charters for the British, Dutch, Germans, Italians and Australians. They made many cruises: Scandinavia, the Black Sea, western Mediterranean, Canary Islands and South Pacific islands. Among the charter operators, the London-based CTC Lines used them for occasional 'line voyages', tourist and migrant trips from London or Southampton to Sydney via the Suez or Panama.

In more recent years, they were laid up on occasion. The *Leonid Sobinov* was idle near Piraeus, Greece, in 1989 together with a small armada of out of work tankers, second-hand banana boats and rusting ferries. There were rumours at the time that an Italian consortium wanted to buy the 608-foot-long ship and turn her into a lavish cruise ship fashioned in the style of the famed Orient Express. After the collapse of the Soviet Union in the summer of 1991, the two ships were transferred to a Maltese-registered holding company, the Transorient Overseas Company.

Above: A far cry from her Cunard days, the *Leonid Sobinov* at Sydney. (*Tim Noble collection*)

Refitted and restyled, the *Carmania* is seen in Valletta harbour in Malta. (*Michael Cassar collection*)

Opposite below, left: Also at Sydney, the *Feodor Shalyapin* returns from a South Seas cruise. (*Tim Noble collection*)
Opposite below, right: The *Carmania* was popular with British cruise travellers as well as Americans. (*Cunard*)

The author saw the *Leonid Sobinov* on one of her last voyages, an extended cruise from St Petersburg around Western Europe and through the Mediterranean to Odessa. Calls en route included Hamburg, Le Havre, Lisbon, Naples and Valletta on Malta (and where your author met the *Shalyapin*). The author also encountered the *Sobinov* at Le Havre. The date was August 1994. By then, the ex-Cunarder was coated in rust streaks, the air conditioning system had broken down, and the outer upper decks were crammed with second-hand cars, mostly German ones, which were bought by Russian passengers for resale back home. Crewmembers in shabby uniforms sold rusted tools, military memorabilia and even empty wine bottles on the quayside. Visitors such as your author were refused entry less for security than the embarrassment of westerners seeing the forlorn state of the interiors.

Afterwards—while the pair was ageing and their owners increasingly short on cash—they managed to run some Mediterranean cruises, sailing out of Odessa to ports as far west as Barcelona. They carried 'domestic' passengers, tourists from the former central Soviet republics who trained in and around Odessa. Subsequent reports by 1995 were that both ex-Cunarders were laid up and in need of considerable repairs. The *Leonid Sobinov* (ex-*Saxonia* and ex-*Carmania*) went to Alang in India in April 1999 to be scrapped; the *Feodor Shalyapin* (ex-*Ivernia* and ex-*Franconia*) followed in February 2004.

The other two sisters, the *Carinthia* and the *Sylvania*, did considerable cruising for Cunard in the 1960s before they too were withdrawn.

Right: A deck plan from the *Carinthia*. (*Andrew Kilk collection*)

Opposite page, clockwise from top left:
Winter cruising on the brand new *Sylvania* in 1957. (*Author's collection*)

The *Sylvania* maintained the Liverpool-Cobh-New York run for several years after the *Britannic* was retired in 1960. (*ALF collection*)

The *Carinthia* seen at New York's Pier 90 in a photograph dated 27 January 1960. (*Gillespie-Faber collection*)

Christmas and New Year's
CRUISE
TO THE
WEST INDIES AND
CENTRAL AMERICA
DECEMBER 21ST 1957

IN THE NEW
SYLVANIA

Left: The handsome 608-foot-long *Carinthia* underway. (*ALF collection*)

Right: The last of the quartet, the *Sylvania* arrives in New York for the first time in December 1957. (*Moran Towing & Transportation Co.*)

The *Sylvania* was repainted in white in her final Cunard years. Historically, the *Sylvania* also made Cunard's last Liverpool-New York crossing in November 1966 and then the *Carinthia* ended the company's Canadian passenger service altogether in October 1967. She also made the company's very last passenger sailing, a cruise, from Liverpool.

The *Carinthia* and *Sylvania* were sold in the winter of 1968 to the Sitmar Line to become the *Fairland* (soon changed to *Fairsea*) and *Fairwind*, and intended for Europe-Australia and around the world passenger services. Ideas soon changed, however, and the ships were lavishly rebuilt as cruise ships: the 910-berth *Fairsea* and *Fairwind*. Completely modernised, they became well known in North American service sailing to Alaska, Mexico, the Caribbean, and on trans-Panama Canal voyages. When Sitmar Cruises was sold to P&O and integrated into their Princess Cruises division in 1988, they passed over to them, becoming the *Fair Princess* and *Dawn Princess* respectively.

The *Fair Princess* (ex-*Carinthia* and ex-*Fairsea*) was to have been sold in October 1995 to Greece's Regency Cruises to become the *Regent Isle*; however, the company went bankrupt before the final transfer was made. Instead, the then thirty-nine-year-old ship was dispatched to lay up at Mazatlan, Mexico, to await resale. A Florida-based group was said to be interested in the former Cunarder for use as a 'casino ship'. Instead, the *Dawn Princess* was transferred to P&O Cruises in Australia and refitted for South Pacific cruising from Sydney mostly. She was finally sold in 2000 to Taiwanese-owned China Seas Cruises, renamed *China Sea Discovery* and eventually used for short gambling cruises out of Keelung. Her days were numbered, however. She was 'arrested' for debt, seized and laid-up, and finally auctioned to Indian scrap merchants. She was scrapped in the winter of 2005–2006. The *Dawn Princess* (ex-*Sylvania* and ex-*Fairwind*) was sold by Princess Cruises in 1992 to the V Group of Monte Carlo and used under charter by Germany's Phoenix Reisen as the *Albatros*. She was decommissioned ten years later in December 2003, but soon sold to Indian shipbreakers. She reached Alang in January 2004 as the provisionally renamed *Genoa*, flying the Georgian flag.

Chapter Twelve

THE MOST FAMOUS LINER IN THE WORLD
Queen Elizazbeth 2

The *Queen Elizabeth 2*, the *QE2* as she is undoubtedly best known, has been the most publicised liner of all time. She has made more newspaper headlines, featured in more television news broadcasts and documentaries, and been the subject of more articles in newspapers as well as magazines than any other passenger ship. In the mid-1990s, she had a starring role in the four-hour television series *The Floating Palaces*. She was also featured in another, also four hours, from Australia and called *The Liners*. A great part of her celebrity was due to her status since she was thought to be the last Atlantic superliner, possibly the very last big ship for historic Cunard and most likely the last *Queen*. Of course, the decision to build the far larger *Queen Mary 2* came in 1998 and she was commissioned in 2004.

After her royal launching at the John Brown shipyard (then renamed Upper Clyde Shipbuilders) on 20 September 1967 and then a delayed maiden crossing in May 1969, noted ocean liner author John Malcolm Brinnin wrote an extended and enthusiastic piece on the new ship for *Holiday* magazine. 'The 963-foot *QE2*, slightly smaller than the two previous *Queens*, was a radical departure from all previous Cunard liners. The new flagship, with her unconventional funnel device, did not even wear the company's familiar colours in black and orange-red. Instead, the name Cunard was painted in red letters along her forward superstructure just below the bridge section. Within, the veneers, oversized leatherettes and English chintzes were replaced by sleek creations of chrome and aluminium, vinyl,

Formica and even plastic. There were two pools on deck, a disco, a gambling casino, at least three different restaurants and a coffee shop, an arcade of shops and a sheltered courtyard on the uppermost deck. The *QE2* was said to be the turning point in ocean liner design and decoration, done in a theme enhanced by Cunard's advertising campaign of the time: "Ships have been boring long enough."'

The author well recalls that overcast day in May when she first sailed into New York's Lower Bay. We were not quite sure what to expect. She was said to look radically different—and she did.

The brand new *France* (on the left) and then the *Mauretania* and *Queen Elizabeth* in this 1962 scene at New York. (*Port Authority of New York & New Jersey*)

Bound for Dubai in November 2008. (*Cunard*)

The maiden arrival of the *Queen Elizabeth 2* in New York's Lower Bay in May 1969. (*David Powers collection*)

Operation *Liner* was held in June 1977 as seven liners departed in a two-hour period. From left to right are the *Statendam*, *Queen Elizabeth 2*, *Doric*, *Oceanic*, *Rotterdam*, *Cunard Princess* and *Kazakhstan*. (*Port Authority of New York & New Jersey*)

To some, they would grow to like her in time; others were crushed in that all-white funnel contraption (itself the bone of some contention) did not even wear those ever so familiar Cunard colours: the red-orange and the double and triple black stripes. Earlier in September 1967 and then in October 1968, your author was aboard specially chartered Circle Line craft, which joined the flotillas that sent off the *Queen Mary* and *Queen Elizabeth*.

We watched, watery-eyed, as two of the most beloved, best looking ocean liners of all time sailed off into the maritime sunset. Some resented the *QE2*. They felt she was the reason that cherished earlier pair of liners was gone (and to the undignified uncertainties of exile in southern California and southern Florida). But just the same on that May afternoon, tugs honked, fireboats sprayed and helicopters buzzed overhead. It was, in fact, the last great maiden voyage show that New York would put on for a new liner and not repeated for another thirty-five years until the maiden arrival of the *Queen Mary 2* in April 2004. Extra tugs assisted as the *QE2* was moved into the south berth of old Pier 92. Headlines read 'The Royal Push' that evening and so it seemed every tug captain wanted his little piece of history. That night, radiant in her lighted decks, windows, portholes and illuminated funnel, extra searchlights played on the new flagship.

An almost 1930s style to modern day advertising and promotion. (*Cunard*)

CUNARD

THE MOST FAMOUS OCEAN LINERS IN THE WORLD

Other big Atlantic legends soon slipped into the uncertainty of early retirement: the *United States* in 1969, the *France* five years later, and then the *Michelangelo* and *Raffaello* in 1975. Somehow and despite the occasional news report to the contrary, the *QE2* managed to endure. She would spend half the year on the old Atlantic run, crossing between Southampton and New York, and with occasional calls at Cherbourg. The rest of the year, she cruised to Bermuda, the Caribbean, the Mediterranean, Norway, and an annual three-month trip around the world. A long list of loyalists adored her. Even well into old age, one couple made eight cruises on her in a single year. The interest, prestige and newsworthiness remained and later increased. A maiden call at Genoa, Italy, in October 1995, for example, drew thousands to the harbour.

Cunard first thought of a third superliner, a replacement for the *Queen Mary*, as far back as the late 1950s. The planning emerged as a traditional, three-class ship that was soon dubbed Q3. There was considerable rethinking, however, by 1962–63, especially in view of the dramatic inroads made by the airlines.

Outbound from New York with the iconic World Trade Center towers in the background. (*Cunard*)

Cruising had to be at least a half-year alternative and perhaps even the crossings had to be more cruise-like, more like holidays in themselves. And so a new project, the *Q4*, emerged. She was ordered in 1965 and just as alternate plans were being made to retire the like of the *Mauretania*, *Caronia* and, most notably, the *Queen Mary*. At this time, ideas were still in place to keep the *Queen Elizabeth* around until as late as 1975. It was planned for her to be the companion to the new superliner until then. A second new superliner, it was said, would be considered in the early 1970s.

The *QE2* in Dubai in March 2010. (*Author's collection*)

BIBLIOGRAPHY

Miller, William H.,
Under the Red Ensign: British Passenger Liners of the '50s & '60s
(Gloucestershire: The History Press, 2009)

Miller, William H.,
The Last Atlantic Liners
(London: Conway Maritime Press Ltd, 1985)

Miller, William H.,
The Last Blue Water Liners
(London: Conway Maritime Press Ltd, 1986)

Newall, Peter,
Cunard Line: A Fleet History
(Preston: Ships in Focus Publications, 2013)

The mighty *Queen Mary 2* in the large graving dock at the Blohm + Voss Shipyard in Hamburg during an overhaul and refit. (*Cunard*)

The great and grand tradition of crossing continues—the towering, 2,600-passenger *Queen Mary 2* passes under New York's Verrazano-Narrows Bridge as she heads off on another week-long passage to Southampton. (*Cunard*)